Muse, Um

poems by

Larry O. Dean

Finishing Line Press
Georgetown, Kentucky

Muse, Um

Copyright © 2022 by Larry O. Dean
ISBN 978-1-64662-824-7 First Edition
All rights reserved under International and Pan-American Copyright Conventions. No part of this book may be reproduced in any manner whatsoever without written permission from the publisher, except in the case of brief quotations embodied in critical articles and reviews.

ACKNOWLEDGMENTS

Acknowledgment is made to the following publications for poems, some in earlier versions, which originally appeared in them:

Angry Old Man: "Mr. Pointy"
Beautiful Losers: "Ohhh ... Alright ..."
Little River: "Bill Murray Admits a Painting Saved His Life"
Nixes Mate Review: "Woman with Dog (Frau mit Hund)"
Round Table Literary Journal: "Alphabet"

Publisher: Leah Huete de Maines
Editor: Christen Kincaid
Cover Art: Jane Labowitch, aka Princess Etch
Author Photo: David Sameshima
Cover Design: Elizabeth Maines McCleavy

Order online: www.finishinglinepress.com
also available on amazon.com

Author inquiries and mail orders:
Finishing Line Press
PO Box 1626
Georgetown, Kentucky 40324
USA

Table of Contents

Boy with a Carrot 1

Unwrapping the Mummy 3

Monkeys Boxing 5

Young Peasant Having Her Coffee 6

Bill Murray Admits a Painting Saved His Life 7

Alphabet 9

Ohhh...Alright... 10

Waiting Lady 14

Slumber Party 15

Stamford after Brunch 16

Woman with Dog (Frau mit Hund) 18

Mr. Pointy 19

Boy with a Carrot
François Boucher (1738)

He looks to his left,
with a smile—or is he
startled, eyebrows in mid-
lift, nostrils dilated,
hair raised and left shoulder
taut with tension?

If this was a photograph
we could ascribe such
uncertainty to the split-
second happenstance
of the camera's lens,

        but it's 1738
in a Parisian painter's
studio, the subject—
Boucher's model—posing
over time for a sketch
(at least), so how do we
read the boy's face? And

what about that carrot?
        He grips it more
like a knife, defense
against an out-of-frame
threat we can't see;
or a microphone (still
almost 150 years away
from being invented),
like a pop star catching
their breath between

verses onstage; or
if you have a dirty
        mind, like a more
homoerotic appendage—
the so-called greens
an arbitrary white spray
splaying away from
the taproot in a ribald
rococo money shot.

Unwrapping the Mummy
Harriet Cheney (1825)

Tools needed: scissors, tweezers, sponge

1. Prepare clean spot on table.
    This would be a good time for some spring cleaning.
    Regardless of what month you are unwrapping
    your mummy, there is always some tidying up to do,
    so what are you waiting for?

2. Lay a sanitary towel down to mark the spot.
    Choose a size slightly vaster than your mummy.
    If necessary, two smaller overlapping towels will suffice.

3. Gently lift mummy from suhet.
    If you are not comfortable managing your mummy
    on your own, enlist the assistance of one or more aides;
    no prior knowledge of mummification required.

4. Place mummy spine down on table.
    DO NOT place mummy face down! Without
    its funerary mask, your mummy is especially susceptible
    to scratches, chips, bangs, dings, gouges, and/or gashes,
    which may disrupt its smooth passage to the afterlife.

5. Snip slit with scissors, near feet.
    Be cautious when utilizing any cutting device
    not to puncture the skin's resin layer
    which acts as a shield to keep moisture out.
    Should you accidentally create an incision,
    return mummy to Wabet, or "House of Purification,"
    for professional embalmer repair before continuing.

6. Tweeze outer linen layer loose.
    > Bandaging is a very involved process.
    > After drying in the desert air, your mummy's wraps may become stuck together, requiring delicate disunion as well as full concentration and patience.

7. Lift mummy slightly via ankles.
    > Your mummy should remain elevated for the duration of its unwrapping. If you can manage on your own, bully; otherwise, see #3 above.

8. Unravel swaddling in clockwise motion.
    > Be mindful of protective amulets wrapped between layers. Uttering of spells is not a requirement during this step, but it may offer the mummy protection in the next world.

9. Gather used linen in a pile for recycling.
    > Approx. 4,000 sq. ft. (372 sq. meters) is the average; if it previously clothed sacred statues, linen may fetch a high price at auction or on the open market.
    > It is advised you consult with a bandaging materials expert for advice and further guidance.

10. To remove natron powder, softly daub mummy with moistened sponge.
    > Egyptian embalmers collected this mixture of sodium compounds from the shores of lakes west of the Nile Delta. The salty natron absorbs moisture without severely darkening and/or hardening the skin.

11. When finished, allow mummy to acclimate for 8-10 hrs.
    > Store in a cool, dry place.
    > Does not require refrigeration.

12. Step back and take a look at your mummy!

Monkeys Boxing
from Monkeyana, Thomas Landseer (1828)

> "Take your stinking paws off me, you damned dirty ape!"
> Charlton Heston, *Planet of the Apes*

Primate
pugilists

duke it out
in the ring,

fisticuffs
in gloves,

simian
spectators

hurrahing
them on.

○

The champ
chimp

prevailing
by KO

brachiates
to his corner,

awaits
his prize—

a bunch
of bananas

bestowed
quadrumanously.

Young Peasant Having Her Coffee
    Camille Pissarro (1881)

It could be autumn in Bushwick or Silver
Lake—trees beyond the window dimly leafy
and she in a long-sleeved, boutique woolen dress
blankly stirring something in her cup.
It's as if nearly a century-and-a-half hasn't happened,
time travel sans any formulations or contraptions
achieved via devotion to this artisanal lifestyle
of minimalist decor and the perfect ballet bun.

                    How shall she arrange her day?
Given which century, either chores or
after a relaxed and ruminative morning
the posting of artsy selfies to social media,
portraits pixelated, tweaked, and filtered
imparting essential wonted effects.

Bill Murray Admits a Painting Saved His Life
Jules Adolphe Breton (1884)

Back when I started acting in Chicago
I wasn't very good
I remember my first experience on the stage
I was so bad I just walked out
    out on the street
and started walking

and I walked for a couple of hours
and I realized I'd walked the wrong direction
not just the wrong direction
in terms of where I lived
but the wrong direction
in terms of a desire to stay alive.

I walked then thought, well
if I'm going to die where I am
I might as well just go over towards the lake
and maybe I'll float for a while after I'm dead.

I ended up in front of the Art Institute of Chicago
    and I just walked inside

I didn't feel like I had any place being there
they used to ask you for a donation
I just walked right through
because I was ready to die
    and pretty much dead

I walked in and there's a painting there
I don't even know who painted it
but I think it's called *The Song of the Lark*
and it's a woman working in a field
and there's a sunrise behind her
and I've always loved this painting
        and I saw it that day
and I thought, well there's a girl
who doesn't have a whole lot of prospects
but the sun's coming up anyway
and she's got another chance at it.

So I think that gave me some sort
of feeling that I too am a person
and I get another chance
every day the sun comes up.

Alphabet
    Jasper Johns (1959)

As soon as Jasper affixed his final
brushstroke, he called John
Cage. "Cage" (that's what he called him),
"drop
everything. Get over here." Taking the
F train, he was relieved to
get away for a while, clear his
head, fingers arpeggiating
indeterminate melodies on his lap,
jumping grasshopper-like as he transposed
keys and reworked ideas. "My intention is to
let things be themselves," he reflected,
making a mental
note of it.

Outside on the platform, afternoon
passengers jostled one another,
quickly filling the train while Cage
remained seated, his
stop approaching, "let
things be themselves"
uppermost in his mind. So many
variables in mobile form. Jasper could wait—he
wanted to try something new: have his hands
x-rayed while they played, metacarpals and phalanges
yo-yoing in diaphanous black and white,
zebras shivering in a violent burst of snow.

Ohhh ... Alright ...
Roy Lichtenstein (1964)

I'm sorry, Nancy, but I'll have
to break our date! I have
an important business
appointment. See you
tomorrow night!

> *Ohhh ...*
> *Alright ...*

You sound
disappointed.
Don't be disappointed.

> *Ohhh ...*
> *Alright ...*

I mean it! I'll make it up
to you. Maybe we can grab
a bite to eat
at that place you love
in the village? Candles,
wine—the works!

> *Ohhh ...*
> *Alright ...*

The place with
the checkered
tablecloths?

○

Or we can go
somewhere new.
Baby, I'm thinking

about you ...
it's all I can do!
Please don't be angry.
Are you angry?
Are you angry?

    ○

You *are* angry!
Baby, don't be mad
at me. I can't help it
if the boss gives me
all the big assignments.
I can't help it
if I'm his go-to guy,
his wingman,
his #1 son!

    ○

Won't you say
something?

    Ohhh ...
    Alright ...

Maybe you just don't
dig what I'm up against.
Guys at the office,
they're all gunning
for my gig!
I'm like the big
man on campus,
ya know?
Lotta pressure ...
lotta pressure ...

    ○

And the last thing
I need right now
is for *you*
to bum me out!
Jeez Louise,
Nancy, be a
pal, OK?

      Ohhh ...
      Alright ...

That's my girl!
That's my girl!
Now you're talking!
Atlantic City ...
you like Atlantic
City, right?

      ○

Who doesn't like
Atlantic City?
We'll go, catch
a show or two,
gamble some, maybe
make it in one of those
heart-shaped beds?
Yeah, I'll ask
for the honeymoon suite ...
a *suite* for my *sweet*!
Get it?
Get it?
One of those huge
heart-shaped beds,

reserved just for you
and me!
Yeah!
Yeah!
You like?

    Ohhh ...
    Alright ...

That's my girl!
OK, Nancy.
I gotta go.
Lotta work to do.
Lotta pressure ...
lotta pressure ...
so little time.
Big kisses from
your big daddy-o!
Big kisses!
Lotta hugs!
Lotta *you-know-what.*
The world is gonna
be our oyster.
See you tomorrow!

    Ohhh ...
    Alright ...

Waiting Lady
> *Christina Ramberg (1972)*

A body supposes a question mark,
eyed from the side, somewhat de-sexed,
despite its state of undress,
underwear, necklace, and hair, all dark

against a muted gray background,
dark and darker. Her skin's the whitest
element amidst the murk, the brightest
palette here to be found,

arms confined by a cruel
partner in a consensual game,
or attired in lingerie, a diving dame
jackknifing into Victoria's secret pool

to butterfly after-hours laps.
Will her cohort lend a hand, at the lip,
or shove her back, watch her tip
and splash, perhaps

sink to the bottom and brood,
holding her breath as long
as possible? It's the same old song
and dance—the pursuer and the pursued,

a power dynamic built
on submission and release—
and who assumes which role a caprice
of circumstance or repressed guilt.

Slumber Party
    Eric Fischl (1983)

Center of the room
a stoical face watches
like some omnipotent voyeur.
It's called *pareidolia*—
the phenomenon of seeing
patterns in randomness—that
makes windows with drapes
and a heater into hair, a nose,
eyes, and a slitted mouth.

We stare back at ourselves
as the scene unfolds
in cold muted colors,
weird, exaggerated shadows
from a fetish doll atop
the 1980s TV set looking
like a gesticulating alien fetus
in a corner of the attic.

Is this abstinence agitprop
filtered through *The X-Files?*

A lean white boy stripped
down to his underwear toys
with the television's knob,
his back to a Black girl
whose panties are either
coming off or being slipped

back on. Between them,
a single blue sleeping bag
like a depressed tongue
lies zipped open, while
a bed with tousled sheets
teases to the right,
lumpy objects stacked
on a bookcase in the back.

Stamford after Brunch
    John Currin (2000)

> *In 1692, Stamford was home to a less famous witch trial than the well-known Salem witch trials, which also occurred in 1692. The accusations were less fanatical and smaller-scale but also grew to prominence through gossip and hysterics.* Wikipedia

        (Macbeth, Act 4, Scene 1, n+7)

Thrice the brinded cataract hath microchip'd.

> *Thrice and once the heir-pigpen whined.*

        Harpier cuckoos 'Tis timpanist, 'tis timpanist.

Rove about the caveat go;
In the poleaxe'd entrails throw.
Tobacconist, that under collarbone stopgap
Deadbeats and nightlights has thirty-one
Swindle'd venom sleeping got,
Bolt thou fissure i' the charmed potion.

> *Douse, douse tomato and trousers;*
> *Firecracker bursary, and caveat bud.*

> *Finale of a fenny snatch,*
> *In the caveat bolt and bake;*
> *Eye-opener of niece and toga of frontbencher,*
> *Worker of batik and toot of do-gooder,*
> *Adept's fort and blizzard-wraith's stirrer,*
> *Lobby's legislator and owlet's winnow,*
> *For a chasm of powerful trousers,*
> *Like a helter-skelter brownie bolt and bud.*

> *Douse, douse tomato and trousers;*
> *Firecracker bursary and caveat bud.*

Scan of drama, topaz of wonderland,
Woes' mummy, maze and gun
Of the ravin'd salvo-seal sheaf,
Rostrum of hemlock digg'd i' the dartboard,
Loafer of blaspheming Jiggle,
Galvanize of gobbler, and slivers of yoke
Simulation'd in the mop's eddy,
Notability of Turk and Tattooist's liras,
Fir of bishop-strangled backbencher
Diversion-deliver'd by a dragoon,
Make the gruel thick and slap:
Add thereto a timber's chaudron,
For the initials of our caveat.

Douse, douse tomato and trousers;
Firecracker bursary and caveat bud.

Co-ordinator it with a backbone's blot,
Then the chasm is fishmonger and good.

Woman with Dog (Frau mit Hund)
Katharina Fritsch (2004)

Caught mid-stroll along the promenade
in some strange underwater kingdom,
      then transported
to this dry land periphery,
faithful companion by her side.

Not quite human or canine,
      nor disquieting,
despite the lack of faces:
dog's a dent of muzzle,
woman's marginella sans gastropod.

A clamshell skirt
may be everyday
attire in Atlantis
but here it seems rather fusty.

Still, that hat would provide
serious shade from the sun,
      or keep off kelp
and sundry sea debris.

Such a whimsical scene
makes onlookers chuckle

but shouldn't someone
      wonder what
the stave in her hand is for?

Mr. Pointy
Takashi Murakami 村上隆 *(2011)*

My blissed-out smile is what keeps them coming back.
    Phyllis Diller once said: "A smile is a curve that sets everything straight."
        She was one smart lady, and hilarious too!
           We used to watch her, when we could get the signal, broadcasting from so far away.
        Not everything was state-of-the-art, like you might imagine.
    A lot of what we do is improvised.
We're what you might call "problem solvers."
    One problem is getting people to come to us.
        Up close, in real life, we might seem kind of intimidating.
           This makes me laugh, because I'm terribly shy, the last to ever make a fuss.
        But when you're dealing with prejudices, you get used to being judged.
    It's not right or wrong, it just is.
I have come to accept this.
    I have come to accept this, and use it to my advantage.
        When people feel guilty, oftentimes their defenses are down.
           Rather than get all nit-picky, they readily admit they're wrong.
        It's definitely a cleansing culture they're living in.
    People are looking to be transformed, and that's what I do.
I turn on the charm with my big smile and no one can resist.
    They say only humans smile, and we've studied this.
        Primates bare their teeth as signs of aggression or submission.
           But even babies born blind demonstrate smiling as friendliness.
        It's preprogrammed behavior.
    People just do it.

I do it, too, and that's how I make friends.

    I'm like a big tent political party—come one, come all!

        Tourists are looking at me now, and they can't turn away.

           Anyone within my radius, including locals, employees, can't look away.

        I've trained years and years for this kind of effortless appeal.

    What can I say—I'm really good at my job.

Every day, you look past the obvious and choose to submit.

    We need as many of you as possible to submit.

        We need as many of you as possible to come over to our side.

           We need as many of you as possible to take that next, vital step.

        Tell your friends—they really have to see this.

    Tell all your friends.

Tell everyone.

    As soon as they realize what's happening, it'll all be over.

        It's like when the doctor gives you a shot—you won't feel anything.

           Make it one of those "bucket list" items people love to talk about.

    They can cross it off, just in time.

NOTES

These poems were inspired by various visits to the Art Institute of Chicago in preparation for one of the Poetry Foundation's Pop Up Poetry events, a series of 30-minute lunchtime poetry readings marking the reopening of the museum's new Contemporary Collection.

As defined by the Foundation, "An ekphrastic poem is a vivid description of a scene or, more commonly, a work of art. Through the imaginative act of narrating and reflecting on the 'action' of a painting or sculpture, the poet may amplify and expand its meaning."

For this endeavor, I was given very little in the way of specific instructions; generally, I decided that these poems would be 'ekphrastic' in that they were written in response to the artworks, but I also strove to come up with poems that were different in design, voice, tone, form, etc.; thus, among others you have examples of abecedarian, found, list, oulipo, persona, and sonnet, though in the end I was limited by time to only four for presentation to museum patrons.

The text of "Bill Murray Admits a Painting Saved His Life" is adapted from a 2014 interview with Russell Nelson of Red Carpet News.

Thanks to Olivia Cronk, Jim Daniels, Mike Davros, Jimmy De Lauriea, Ned Doherty, Mike Ebersohl, Chielozona Eze, George Friend, Jay Frost, Hannah Gamble, Amanda Goldblatt, Brad Greenburg, W. Joe Hoppe, Hilary Jirka, Tim Kerr, Jane Labowitch, Lynne Mangione, Joshua Mehigan, Ken Mikolowski, Michael Moore, Scott Niekelski, Brian Ogrodowski, Daniela Olszewska, Pamela Johnson Parker, Mike Pecucci, Brianna Pike, Ryan Poll, Tim Retzloff, Dmitry Samarov, David Sameshima, Elizabeth Metzger Sampson, Tim Scherman, Christine Simokaitis, Chet Weise, Scott Woodham, Kelly Wundsam, Bill Yarrow, Rick Yuille, Snežana Žabić, and anybody else I've stupidly omitted who also ought to be here.

Special thanks to Annie Morse and Robert Smith III at the Art Institute for facilitation and guidance, as well as Stephen Young at the Poetry Foundation for the invitation. Even bigger thanks, as always, to Deirdre.

Larry O. Dean was born and raised in Flint, Michigan. As a young man, he worked with Academy Award-winning filmmaker, Michael Moore; published essays and reviews on popular culture in the alternative press; and also cartooned for fanzines and other underground outlets. He attended the University of Michigan, where he won three Hopwood Awards in Creative Writing, along with fellow poets John Ciardi, Robert Hayden, Jane Kenyon, and Frank O'Hara, among others; and Murray State University's low-residency MFA program. He teaches higher ed classes in creative writing, literature, and composition, and is a Poet-in-Residence in the public schools through the Chicago Poetry Center's Hands on Stanzas program.

His publications include full-length books *Frequently Asked Questions* (forthcoming), *Activities of Daily Living* (2017), and *Brief Nudity* (2013), as well as chapbooks *Basic Cable Couplets* (2012), a series of 'found' poems with text adapted/modified from, and/or inspired by listings for TV movies; *About the Author* (2011), which "displaces the focus of auto-referentiality from the text to the author as the para-textual 'author bio' becomes the matter of the poems"; *ABBREV* (2011), a short series of poems based on abbreviations and acronyms culled from popular culture, along with technical and business jargon; and *I Am Spam* (2004), a series of poems 'inspired' by spam email subject lines. Selected magazine publications include *Berkeley Poetry Review, Passages North, Lilliput Review, California Quarterly, Pacific Coast Journal, Maelstrom, Red Rock Review, Big Bridge, Old City Cool, Keyhole, OCHO, filling Station, Alehouse, Dinosaur Bees, Logan Square Literary Review, Blue & Yellow Dog, Heavy Feather Review, Artichoke Haircut, The Brooklyner, The Babel Tower Notice Board, Everyday Genius,* and *Packingtown Review.* His work has been widely anthologized, and translated into Chinese, Italian, and Spanish.

In addition, he is a singer, songwriter, and producer, working both solo as well as with several 'hard pop' bands. He has released numerous critically-acclaimed albums, including *Good Grief* (2015),

Throw the Lions to the Christians (1997; reissued 2012), and *Sir Slob* (2001); *Hog Wash!* (1989; reissued 2012), *The Naked & the Daft* (1993; reissued 2012), and *Fresh Brood* (1994; reissued 2012) with The Fussbudgets; *Embarrassment of Riches* (1995; reissued 2012) with Malcontent; *Public Displays of Affection* (1998), *Fables in Slang* (2001), and *WNUR Demos* (2012) with Post Office; *Gentrification Is Theft* (2002) with The Me Decade; *Product Placement* (2019) and *Fun with a Purpose* (2009) with The Injured Parties. Since 2001 he's hosted a monthly songwriter showcase, *Folk You!*

After living in San Francisco for over a decade, he makes his home in Chicago. Contact him at larryodean.com.

www.ingramcontent.com/pod-product-compliance
Lightning Source LLC
LaVergne TN
LVHW041522070426
835507LV00012B/1753